4 Faces of Death

Written by
Wayne W. Sanders

Christian Literature & Artwork
A BOLD TRUTH Publication

4 Faces of Death
Copyright © 2017 by Wayne W. Sanders
ISBN 13: 978-0-9991469-6-5

BOLD TRUTH PUBLISHING
(Christian Literature & Artwork)
606 West 41st, Ste. 4
Sand Springs, Oklahoma 74063
www.BoldTruthPublishing.com

Available from Amazon.com and other retail outlets. Orders
by U.S. trade bookstores and wholesalers.
Email *beirep@yahoo.com*

Quantity sales special discounts are available on quantity
purchases by corporations, associations, and others. For
details, contact the publisher at the address above.

Printed in the USA.
10 17   10 9 8 7 6 5 4 3 2 1

We would like to recognize and thank these Publishers, for publishing and distributing the following versions of God's written Word.

The Lord gave the word: great was the company of those that published it. - Psalm 68:11 (KJV)

*"I am the resurrection, and the life:
he that believeth in me, though he were dead,
yet shall he live:"*

- *Jesus Christ*, The Messiah
As recorded in John's Gospel
(c. 30 AD)

Content

Content

Foreword

At first I had thought to tell you (the reader) how the pages of this book read like an adventure novel. But then I began to think about the man who penned the pages of this book, and a little Holy Ghost inspired laughter rose up out of me; because, I realized just being friends with, and being around the ministry of Wayne and Connie Sanders—IS AN ADVENTURE.

Proverbs 11:30 NKJV
The fruit of the righteous is a tree of life, And he who wins souls is wise.

From their once a week Bible Studies at Wayne's ministry headquarters (COMMON GROUND MINISTRIES) to their busy travel schedule, taking ministry teams of men and women out onto the streets of cities all across this nation: (Indianapolis [500]; Houston; New Orleans; Pittsburg; St. Louis; and many more) as well as taking dozens and dozens of trips to Honduras, Central America, Wayne and his team continue to share THE GOOD NEWS OF JESUS CHRIST in song and powerful preaching of The Word—with signs and wonders following.

i

Foreword

I consider Wayne Sanders to be one of my most trusted friends in ministry, as well as a mentor (especially on the subject of public and one-on-one evangelism). The impact he and his team have had on my life and ministry can't simply be recorded here. I'm sure Heaven's record will show many lives that have been touched (through other ministries) because of Wayne's continual encouraging, mentoring and setting the pace through example.

I am both blessed and excited about my involvement with the publishing of this book. It is a wonderful TESTIMONY to the One Who gives all things life. You know, our God is not dead. He is alive and well: He is a SUPERNATURAL BEING exercising His will and plans over any situation, logic or natural law—when and where He chooses. JESUS CHRIST IS OUR MIRACLE-WORKER and within the pages of this book you will find abundant evidence of these TRUTHS.

Thank you Wayne for allowing me to be a part of this blessed project. Much love to you and your family!

Aaron Jones
Revivalist, Author and Artist
Sand Springs, Oklahoma

Introduction

It amazes me on how many people go to church ever week that have still not resolved this issue in their lives. Death is not a subject that most people want to talk about, but we will all go that way one day. My doctor told me once that none of us will get out of this life alive.

I am sure that not everything you are seeking answers for will be found in the pages of this book. I don't intend on trying to make you think I have all of the answers. I only hope to provoke you into examining the outcome of these events in the hope of giving you something to help you make a choice which will make your final destination secure.

Jesus said in His Word, in *John 14:1-3*...

> *1 "Let not your heart be troubled: ye believe in God, believe also in me.*
> *2 In my Father's house are many mansions; if it were not so, I would have told you; I go to prepare a place for you.*
> *3 And if I go and prepare a place for you, I will come again, and receive you unto myself; that where I am, there ye may be also."*

Introduction

If you are one of those who refuse to look at the alternative that awaits you in death, then I suggest you put this book back on the shelf. However, if you are searching for some answers that can help you make the most important decision in your life then put a death grip on this book and read it.

The way in which a person perceives death, and then comes to grips in dealing with it: can be altered by the experiences that we have with it.

The definition for *death* can leave us with this lost feeling or hopelessness. Webster's definition says: "death is a permanent cessation of all vital functions: the end of life"

There are all kinds of books and other sources of information one can find on the subject of death. If you are like me though, some of those reports only left me more confused after I read them.

Avoiding the subject of death as long as possible is the way most people prefer to approach it; nevertheless, still one day we will all have to face it. My prayer is: that you will find the answers you are looking for. I can only explain to you what I understand about the subject of death. That's the topic of this book, I'm going to share with you how I view death.

At least twice a year we spend two to three weeks on short-term mission trips in the country of Honduras, Central America. The testimonies that have come out of these unusual and exciting adventures, I have to admit, are sometimes almost unbelievable; but they keep us going back year after year.

Introduction

I have told these experiences many times to my friends and they felt I needed to write some of them down. It has proven to be a little difficult for me to describe them in words and put them in a book like this.

The events I am going to convey to you in the pages of this book are not fictional, or as unbelievable as they may seem. There are twenty-one witnesses who can attest to their authenticity.

Just as the books of the Gospels share the same theme but are viewed from four different perspectives, even these events, (as viewed through the eyes of each witness,) can be seen from the perspective of that individual's personal life experiences; each account may be told with some variations but with the same truths.

I will try to describe to you as accurately as possible how these chain of events unfolded. I feel compelled to share them with you, even at the risk of being tagged as a lunatic. I want to explain to you just what transpired before coming to Honduras, while on this trip, and even after the conclusion of these events.

There are four different situations that occurred during one of those three week mission trips—they are the reason for this book. These four testimonies will be shared in the sequence they happened to us on that trip.

The first encounter was with a man who was killed on the highway as we were coming back from the waterfalls in Pulhapanzak, on the road going to Rio Lindo, Cortes in

Introduction

the Northern side of Honduras.

The second encounter was a man who was killed on the highway as we were coming back from the city of La Lima, Cortes just 10 miles west of San Pedro Sula.

The third encounter was a man who had died from fear in a city called Ocotepeque, (in western Honduras).

The last encounter was my older brother, Danny, who said he kept waking up all night long thinking he was going to die.

These are the **'4 Faces of Death'** that will be discussed in this book. Obviously there are numerous other encounters we could discuss along these lines, but for the sake of time we will only focus on these for now.

These are the events that happened on our mission trip in the year of 1997.

Wayne W. Sanders

4 Faces of Death

Chapter 1

It Has to Start Somewhere

It was in March, 1997 when we arrived once again in the beautiful country of Honduras. We were all looking forward to experiencing yet another great adventure together, and had been preparing for this trip for several months now.

Making sure all of the arrangements for getting our musical equipment there so we could hold our meetings without having to depend on the churches to provide it for us, was proving to be a difficult task. Just setting up our schedule with the churches could sometimes be exhausting. Not to mention securing a place for us to stay for three weeks. But it all paid off and we were finely there.

We were enjoying one of the cool beautiful summer evenings that are found only on rare occasions in the earlier months of the year. I was grateful to see that it hadn't really been all that hot yet. The weather could change at any moment though, turning this tropical paradise into the blistering and intense conditions that the climate in San Pedro Sula is often noted for.

1

4 Faces of Death

We've been accused by many of our Honduran friends of bringing cold weather into their country with us. They say the temperatures always cool down for us gringos when we show up. It will be in the lower 100's just days before our arrival. Then, seemingly out of nowhere, a cool front will sweep across the city, bringing with it a refreshing rain and cloud cover making it enjoyable and bearable for our stay there.

They will all be running around with sweaters and jackets on while we will be in short sleeve shirts. We are talking about temperatures from the upper 70's into the lower 80's. So it really doesn't bother me if they want to blame us for all the mild weather. I am more than happy to take the blame for this expression of God's love being shown. I just figure that God was showering His wonderful favor upon us.

The gentle breezes coming across the upper deck of our two-story house that first night felt just like the refreshing that comes right after a mild summer rain. The upper deck of the house wrapped itself completely around two sides of it, and proved to be more than adequate enough to hold our prayer meetings on. There were twenty-one men and women from all around the United States who had gathered together here to seek God's will with a fervency and passion.

The house we were staying at was used for the local headquarters of a ministry called *Juventud Para Christo de Honduras*. ("Youth for Christ in English") Two very good friends of ours: Mauricio and Anna Erazo, are the national directors. Lots of prayer had gone up from here, and you could feel the effects from it the moment you entered the house.

Our place of refuge was nestled directly at the bottom of a very large mountain, but was still within the suburbs of the city. You could easily find our place by looking for the large Coca-Cola sign directly above us on the mountainside. *(See photo, p. 10)*

Oh yeah! This house was the perfect place for us to come to. It was a place where we could draw closer to God, and then listen for His instructions. It would be many years later down the road before we would actually realize the significant part of God's plans that had been birthed out of intercession as we prayed out the mysteries and the secrets that were being revealed to us by His Spirit in this awesome place.

The city of San Pedro Sula would soon be revealed to us as a strategic position in the plans God had, not only for the country of Honduras; but on a global perspective as well.

The team for the mission trip had come from the great state of Texas, Missouri, Illinois, Florida, Oklahoma, Ohio, and even Mississippi. So it was necessary for us to get onto the same page if you know what I mean.

Unity played a significant part in the outcome of anything we chose to do together for the Lord. Because of the diversity of the team, we held a mandatory devotional each morning. These devotionals were just as important as the services and meetings held in the churches each night because: "direction brings protection."

The first day everyone was enjoying their time of fellowship together and catching up with news from back home. Getting instructions for the next assignment was the central theme for that day's agenda; this, of course, had released a lot of excitement into the atmosphere.

After our meeting secession I was engaged in an interesting conversation with one of the team members who also happened to be a very good friend of mine. Roger Ward and I met in 1989 in Broken Arrow, Oklahoma and attended the same bible school together. Both Roger and his beautiful wife, Darlene, have accompanied me throughout the years on many other missions' trips as well as working with me in the prison ministry.

He was sharing with me a dream he had earlier that day while taking a nap. He explained, he usually didn't have dreams like this one when he's just taking a short siesta.

He said "I saw you standing in an open space. There was this bright light that was shining down all around you. Just a few short feet away, was this total darkness surrounded you. I struggled to see what was just on the other side of that darkness so I could at least get some kind of idea on where *this was all taking place. I couldn't make out anything, so I suppose you could have been almost anywhere.*

"I asked you what were you doing as you began pointing with your finger into the darkness and speaking to it. You said that you were telling the north to give up their dead. Then you turned to the south, to the east, and to the west repeating the same jesters and commanding the same thing to each of them.

"Oddly enough," Roger said, "I found myself joining in with you, and making the same verbal commands as I too began pointing into the darkness with my finger."

~

***These devotionals were just as important
as the services and meetings
held in the churches each night because:
"direction brings protection."***

Have you ever had one of those moments where it seemed like everything around you just seemed to fade out of sight? That's the way it was that evening standing on the upper deck of that old house as Roger shared his dream with me.

We both found ourselves taking action in light of what was being described to us in the dream. Pointing to the north, south, east and west we made those same verbal commands. We were absolutely sure there had to be some significant meaning to this dream but at the time we would have to just patiently wait and see.

I found this Scripture in the book of Isaiah that seemed to run along the same line of thought as the dream, but at the time I just didn't see how if fit in the puzzle.

It was a promise from God that Israel would be reunited with Him once again at the end of this dispensation. But frankly, I still didn't get it, or understand why Roger said I was calling out for the darkness to give up its dead.

There is the vague understanding that the word *death* does not necessarily mean we cease to exist when we die. Though the outward man perishes in death, our spirit man, or the inward man, if not born again, is separated from God's presence forever. I was guessing he was referring to that kind of separation.

Isaiah 43:5-7
5 Fear not: for I am with thee: I will bring thy seed from the east, and gather thee from the west;
6 I will say to the north, Give up; and to the south, keep not back: bring my sons from far and my daughters from the ends of the earth;
7 Even every one that is called by my name: for I have created him for my glory, I have formed him; yea, I have made him.

4 Faces of Death

I know these Scriptures don't specifically mention the word *"death"* but it does talk about a separation. I felt like I needed to be very careful not to try and pull this Scripture out of its context in order to provide myself with some kind of logical direction out of this odd experience. (A seed will lay dormant until planted into the dirt, and then, when it dies, it breaks forth into life.)

We just had to wait until the Lord saw [it was time] to reveal what it meant to us. I kept praying for a better understanding (revelation) of Roger's dream; nevertheless, for the time being, we just put it up on the shelf so to speak.

The first evening everyone was looking forward to all of the services that had been scheduled for us. Over the next three weeks we provided over seventy services just in the evenings alone.

In addition to all the night services, we were doing morning and afternoon visits to the prisons, school, and hospitals. Crusades were also scheduled in the streets of the city parks, as well as the lower market places–so our days filled up quickly.

We had been warned: some of these places were also very dangerous. Even the police asked us to reconsider some of our services that would be held down in the lower market place.

4 Faces of Death

We were scheduled to go a large church on the first night called *La Cosecha*, which in English means *"The Harvest."* The church is located just on the outskirts of the city; heading towards the airport.

The service was being held under a tent that would seat over 7,000 people. It is an awesome experience to be in the presence of God at one of these huge gatherings. The pastor also had a television station that was broadcasting the service live on the air to an audience estimated to be over a million viewers. On that particular night the tent was filled to capacity and had overflow spilling into the outer darkness just beyond the edges of the tent.

~

A seed will lay dormant until planted into the dirt, and then, when it dies, it breaks forth into life.

When we arrived, the service was already well underway. They brought us up to the front to be seated. There was an energy that filled the atmosphere like electricity and everyone was standing on their feet praising God.

There was singing and shouting. There were hundreds of people that were up at the front of the platform, and they were all dancing with all of their strength before the Lord. What a passion these people have to express love and devotion towards our God! I wish we would see more of that here in our churches (in the States).

Then the pastor began to give instructions to the church; telling some to turn to the north, some to the south, some to the east, and some to the west. He began to point out into the darkness just beyond the tent's edge and gave commands that each direction would give up their dead.

I looked over at Roger and we both began to laugh and rejoice as we entered in with them shouting out the same commands that had been given to us in Roger's dream. The experience we shared on the deck of that old house was now being continued under this magnificent tent as the pastor was passionately pouring out of his spirit, utterances that came directly from the Lord.

I could not wait to see what the Lord had in store for us, but I was not quite prepared for what was to come next. The stage for one of the most spectacular set of events we had ever encountered was set under the direction of the Holy Spirit. Things were now underway to be executed from the realm of the supernatural into the natural realm we now live in.

4 Faces of Death

We stayed at a ministry headquarters
(*Juventud Para Christo de Honduras*) in the city of
San Pedro Sula, Honduras Central America.

4 Faces of Death

Chapter 2

This Was a Set Up

After a few years of going down to Honduras: I believe that we have had enough time to figure a few things out. You know what I mean? A man needs to know when it's time to work and when it's time to rest, right? Back on our first trip down there in 1995, we hit the ground running hard and fast; never once taking time out to look back. By the end of that trip we had very little voices left, and it took us days just to get ourselves back into the swing of things.

Fred Bishop (the founder of No Greater Love Ministries in southern Illinois), had personally invited us to come and help him with his ministry outreach. He had been serving in Honduras for over 25 years and tried to share from his experiences about taking some time out to rest—we didn't want to miss anything though.

Looking back now, I can see we should have reconsidered our own personal opinions on how things ought to have been done, and taken some of his advice. Well you know how it is right? You live and you learn.

So we decided to rent a bus and we were all going to the

beach for some time of rest and relaxation. I was of the opinion we had come here to minister to the Hondurans and not to play. After all we are ministers of the Gospel, right? And we are on a mission's trip, right?

We thought we would be smart and take our sound equipment and instruments to the beach along with us. We thought we could kill two birds with one stone. We could go play and minister at the same time. After arriving at the beach, it took us over an hour just to set up and start playing.

The funny thing was, the only people on the beach that day were the people from our group. Once it [finally] sunk into our brains, we lugged all of our equipment back to the bus and returned to the beach to join in on some of the fun. We got to play in the ocean for just under a half hour before we had to return back to San Pedro Sula to get ready for our evening services. Oh boy, if that wasn't a great letdown!

After learning that lesson we were bound and determined we weren't going to be making the same mistake again. Our day off was going to be our day off to relax.

Two years later we had scheduled a day of rest for the first Monday into our mission trip. We were going to a place with a waterfall in Pulhapanzak on the road going to Rio Lindo, Cortes on the Northern side of Honduras.

We had heard this was one of the most beautiful waterfalls

in the world. Its crystal clear waters flow out of a mountainside into two pools that you can swim in. Then they flow together into a one hundred and forty foot waterfall (which is only some forty feet shorter than our Niagara Falls). The falls drop downward and crash onto the rocks below and then flow into one of the most beautiful rivers; it is said to be a sight for all to see. I could not wait for this time of rest and relaxation.

After learning that lesson we were bound and determined we weren't going to be making the same mistake again.

The first four to five days of our trip were brutal on us as we moved our sound equipment in and out of every meeting or service we did. Sometimes we would hold as many as three services a day; each time we were putting our equipment up and then taking it down.

Keep in mind: the people in Honduras are not interested in having just a one-hour meeting either; some of these meetings would continue on for (three or four hours) at a time; you would almost be begging them to please let you stop.

All of our services consisted of at least one hour to set up. Then we would have worship for at least one hour followed by the message, which would be concluded by praying for the people.

4 Faces of Death

Then it would take another hour just to tear down the equipment and load it back on the bus. Once we got back to the house, we would unload the bus again before falling into our beds, trying to find some time to rest before doing it all over again.

I'm not complaining at all; I just want to show you how exhaustive it can be and how much we were really looking forward to taking a day off to get some much needed rest.

Monday had finally arrived and the bus was loaded, fueled, and ready for the two and a half hour journey that would take us to this wonderful place people talked about so much. Everyone had the choice to stay back at the house, go into the city, or just do whatever he or she wanted on the day off; however, we were all excited about seeing this beautiful place, so the whole team went along that day.

The ride was enjoyable, even though the bus was not really all that comfortable. Just getting out and seeing all of the beautiful countryside along the way and how the people lived there was always very interesting and quite satisfying to me. When we pulled into the park, it was everything that they said it would be and then some.

Some of the local boys that lived in the nearby town greeted us and offered their assistance by giving us a tour. They had a lot of interesting information about the history of this area, so we decided to go with them.

4 Faces of Death

There was a cool, refreshing mist that filled the air as you looked over into this large gaping hole that was being poured into by this enormous stream of water. Our new tour guides asked us if we would like to go into a cave that was located at the bottom on the other side of the falls—I thought that would be awesome. I grew up at the Lake of the Ozarks in Missouri, and felt like it was right up my alley.

It was a long way down this cliff and I could not see a clear path on how we were going to get there. The boys had us jumping off the edge of this cliff over into the top of a tree and then shimming down to the bottom just to do it all over again. Wow! It was a lot of fun: but sort of scary too.

As we were moving in closer to the falls the sound of all the water coming down was almost deafening. It was in [that moment], I began to realize how majestic the Voice of the Lord can be. In *the book of Psalms Chapter 29, verses 3 and 4* it read this way:

> *3 "The voice of the LORD is upon the waters; the God of glory thundereth; the LORD is upon many waters.*
> *4 The voice of the LORD is powerful; the voice of the LORD is full of majesty."*

You could almost hear Him speaking to you those powerful Words, *"I will never leave you nor forsake you, for I am with you always"*.

4 Faces of Death

With the heavy midst and enormous amounts of water that was falling from the top of the cliff would leave you breathless. Literally, you would be gasping for your next breath of air; you would have to turn your back to the falls and bend over while cupping your hands over your mouth as you tried desperately to catch a small shallow breath of air.

I had been loosed from all of the cares of this world as I waded through the rough terrain of the riverbed. We had to maneuver ourselves around large boulders and pools of water that were deep enough to swim in. We were taking our time enjoying the refreshing coolness the afternoon's adventure had provided us.

～

It was in [that moment],
I began to realize how majestic
the Voice of the Lord can be.

In a way, you felt almost isolated from the other team members, even though they were all standing next to you. You were not able to speak to them even if you were screaming because of the tremendous volume of the massive amount of water crashing down around you. But as you slowly moved into the mouth of the cavern, there was a peace that cannot be described in words.

The sound of the waters seemed to fade miles away and there was this quiet hush that settled over everyone as we

16

4 Faces of Death

all sat gazing through the waterfall. How long we stayed there, I really don't remember, but I guarantee you one thing: it was longer than a lifetime of memories.

Now came the most difficult part of this excursion. Just thinking about climbing back up out of this deep hole to the top of the cliffs was not a very pleasant thought.

I told our young guides, this was going to be a very difficult trip up that cliff for some of us. They said, *"That's no problem. There are stairs just around the corner."* I couldn't believe my ears on what I just heard him say! After going through such a treacherous climb down, now we find out there were stairs!

When we got back to the top and back to safety, they then made an announcement that they wanted $25.00 per person for taking us on our little tour. Not understanding their customs I was not very happy, but we did make a settlement for a lot less denarius.

4 Faces of Death

Pulhapanzak Waterfall, Honduras Central America

4 Faces of Death

Chapter 3

The 1st Face of Death
We Didn't See It Coming

All in all it was a tremendous way to spend the day with all of our friends. We got back on our bus and started the descent back down the mountainside. Going through several small towns and villages the road seemed pretty small for our big, old bus to be traveling down.

The first encounter was with a man (who was killed on the highway) as we were coming back from the waterfalls in Pulhapanzak.

Looking out of the window at all the beautiful scenery, it was easy to find yourself caught up with what God had created here. You could almost feel like He had created it just for you.

You could almost hear Him speaking to you those powerful Words, "I will never leave you nor forsake you, for I am with you always".

4 Faces of Death

We were all praising God for the wonderful way He had provided for us all to come to this monumental place when all of a sudden, out of nowhere, there came this little pickup truck past us at a high rate of speed.

The driver went around the bus loaded with 100-pound bags of beans and rice piled as high as he could get onto his truck; the sheer weight of his cargo was more than that little truck could manage. In addition, we were also in a highly populated area and he should have been a little more cautious: there were people walking on both sides of the road, even as narrow as it was.

The truck was swaying from side to side and looked as though it were about to turn over from the weight on top of it. The shocks and springs were so bad, the truck looked as though it was resting on the frame. (They would never allow that situation to occur in the States.)

We went about another half a mile or so down the road when we ran up upon this truck again. The driver had lost control of the vehicle and went off the side of the road into a concrete culvert. There was a small bridge across the culvert where the truck had come to rest. The truck was smashed into it, and was wedged into the corner of the bridge.

It doesn't take long for a crowd to gather when something like this happens; in this case, people had already started to gather around—it seemed like they just appeared out of nowhere. Mauricio was driving the bus and asked if we should stop. Someone hollered out, *"Yes! There is a bicycle sticking out from under the truck."* So we pulled over on the side of the road where we could park.

This tragic situation presented itself to us without any warning: one moment we are praising God and in the next moment we were faced with a dilemma. Shawn opened up the door at the back of the bus and everyone started pouring out into the street to try to help out.

The truck was very heavy with all its cargo and it took several men to rock it backwards. Under it was the rider of the bicycle that had been trapped between the truck and the bridge. They threw his body up on the ground. It looked as though they had just pitched up a bag of potatoes.

We were all still dressed in our swimming suits, but as I started getting down from the bus, I had a strong impression that I should put my pants on over my swimming suit and present myself as a minister [when I heard these words], *"He's dead."* It all seemed to be moving in slow motion; everything taking place in front of me seemed as though it was a horrible scene out of some bad B-rated movie.

By the time I got dressed and off of the bus, a large crowd had already gathered around him. When I walked up on the scene, our guys were already on their knees surrounding him and intensely praying for him. The man's wife and children were standing over him sobbing uncontrollably.

We had one man on our team who was captain of a fire department in New Orleans: he was trained for these kinds of accidents. After examining him, he said the man was dead and there was no oxygen flowing through his blood.

George, another member of our team, was trying to wipe the blood off of the man's face with a handkerchief which he had with him. The drama of the man's family standing right in front of him made a lasting impression upon him and he said that he had gotten caught up in all of the anguish.

The man's head had been crushed and was severely caved in; his jaw was broken and the bottom part of his mouth was turned sideways; his right chest and shoulder were also crushed and he had sustained multiple crushing blows to the rest of his body; also, with all of the cuts he had there was a tremendous amount of blood loss.

It is very tragic to witness this kind of thing. No matter what may be going on with you at the time, it seems like you are never prepared for it. Even when you know that something is going to happen, you still have to deal with the shock of it.

What happened next was absolutely incredible. As we were praying you could sense this presence that seemed to fill the atmosphere. You know that feeling right before someone takes a picture with a flashcube? In that moment you would blink your eyes and even turn away from the bright light in an involuntary motion. Well that's exactly what happened to me.

I turned my head for just a second and when I looked back, the man was sitting straight up. His head and face were back to normal along with his chest and shoulder. He spit some blood out of his mouth and asked what happened. One moment the man was lying on the ground dead and the next moment he was sitting up and looked perfectly normal!

~

As we were praying you could sense this presence that seemed to fill the atmosphere.

Someone asked me later if I got a chance to preach to the crowd while I had them all there. I said to them, *"What was I going to say? I saw the same thing that they saw."*

At a much later time, I was sharing this incredible testimony and someone said to me he didn't believe it was possible that the man was raised from the dead. *"I know that it is hard to believe that someone could be raised up from the dead,"* I replied to him, *"But if he wasn't dead, he defiantly was severely mangled; and God restored him back to normal in front of all those witnesses."*

I told him I had just witnessed one of the most powerful

and miraculous sermons I'd ever heard or seen preached. There is no man who could have ever preached that good of a message except for Jesus Christ Himself; along with His sermon—He gave a living illustration. The crowd went from weeping to raising their hands up in the air and praising Jesus for what He had just done.

They didn't need anyone to tell them what had just occurred. They were already giving credit to Jesus for this wonderful display of compassion and mercy without anyone giving them their (opinion) about what they had just witnessed.

There was a doctor passing by that stopped to examine the situation. Several men picked the man up off of the ground, and as they carried him away, he was still in a sitting position. He was protesting about being taking away to a hospital. They put him in the back of a truck and drove away with the man still insisting he was okay and that nothing was wrong with him.

As we got back aboard the bus we were all almost speechless. It took us over an hour from this point to get back to the house. There was not much talking going on in the bus and one man, Frank—wept all the way back home.

I have heard of things like this happening, but to be a firsthand witness can be very sobering. As you can imagine there were a lot of unanswered questions about what just happened.

4 Faces of Death

Once we arrived back at the house, everyone started talking a mile a minute trying to explain what they saw. I felt really compelled to tell everyone to just go to bed and let the Lord speak to them that night. Then in the morning, when we got up, we would examine the evidence and write it down just as we saw it unfold.

I wasn't sure how everybody else fared trying to get to sleep that night, but I had a hard time digesting what I had witnessed that day; I prayed there would be peace for all of us. Wake up call in the morning was going to come with some very unusual chain of events, that I was sure of. There was a great mystery that had been displayed before us, and many of us were going to have to make some drastic changes in our patterns of believing.

There was one thing that I thought about a lot was how normal this unbelievable event felt. It was almost like this is just the way it is supposed to be done. There was no eerie feeling like I was in the twilight zone or something like that. I prayed for the morning to hurry up and come.

I'm not so sure what the time was when I finally dozed off to sleep, but when I woke up the next morning I had a huge desire that was like a flame of fire that was ready to be satisfied with some sort of relief.

4 Faces of Death

Chapter 4

All Things Are Possible
To Him Who Believes

That morning the house was filled with excitement as everyone gathered around in the dining room for breakfast. Laughter and giggling broke through the silence of the night with an anticipation you would expect to find in little school kids on Christmas morning.

Everyone was ready to just skip breakfast and get on with the discussion of these incredible events. We needed God to help direct the meeting so we could write down all the details in order to get a reliable description that we could relate to, as well as, pass it on to others.

I started sharing what I saw, *"I remember coming across the bridge and seeing the man lying on the ground with his wife and children standing over him sobbing. Several members of the team had already positioned themselves around the man and were praying over him. Hundreds of people were gathering all around us kneeling down beside him looking for any signs of life."*

Joe, who was the fire captain from New Orleans, explained

4 Faces of Death

that oxygen to the blood causes it to coagulate and then turn red, but his blood was blue. He said he also found no pulse and no sign of life.

Frank never said anything that day, but later said he felt this power go through him: he couldn't talk all the way back to the house. I guess even now we will probably never know all that took place that day.

As we continued to share what happened, George said he heard the Lord speaking to him, telling him to grab the man by the toes. He thought about how silly that sounded and said he was so caught up with the scene in front of him that he found himself trying to wipe the blood of the man's face, as he was frantically looking into the faces of this man's wife and children.

Then Shawn told us the Lord had spoken to him also and told him to grab the man by the toes, so he obeyed and did it. It was at this time in the conversation that George realized somebody else had heard God tell them to do the same thing. He sat and wept thanking God someone had heard the Voice of God and then obeyed.

What I witnessed next was indescribable. I told the group *"It was like a spark or a flash from a camera which caused me to turn away for just a second. When I looked back the man sat straight up. His face was completely back to normal, his shoulder and chest were back to normal. He spit*

4 Faces of Death

some blood out of his mouth and asked what happened!

"One moment the man was lying on the ground dead and the next moment he was sitting up and looked perfectly normal, except he still had the blood on his clothes; which was evidence of the terrible accident that had just happened moments before.

"The crowd immediately went from crying to rejoicing and giving praise to God for this tremendous miracle they all witnessed in front of them. A doctor stopped by and they picked the man up, carried him to the road, and put him in the back of a pickup truck. He kept insisting that nothing was wrong with him, as they drove away."

With that, we were launched into a series of events that would cause me to look deeper for answers about the dream Roger had and what we had just experienced with this man. When you see something as dramatic as this–the mind wants to deny it. I am a Christian and I look for my answers to come from and out of the Word of God.

Here are some things I was able to sort out that helped me to better understand this amazing story.

This first experience of the **4 Faces of Death** we encountered on this trip, showed me that, even when you tell someone about this incredible experience you had—most people will call you a bald-face liar because they can't believe it's possible.

4 Faces of Death

Even our bus driver who had witnessed this whole chain of events with his own eyes said that the first man could not have been dead.

~

One moment the man was lying on the ground dead and the next moment he was sitting up and looked perfectly normal...

Luke 16:19-31 KJV
19 There was a certain rich man, which was clothed in purple and fine linen, and fared sumptuously every day:
20 And there was a certain beggar named Lazarus, which was laid at his gate, full of sores,
21 And desiring to be fed with the crumbs which fell from the rich man's table: moreover the dogs came and licked his sores.
22 And it came to pass, that the beggar died, and was carried by the angels into Abraham's bosom: the rich man also died, and was buried;
23 And in hell he lift up his eyes, being in torments, and seeth Abraham afar off, and Lazarus in his bosom.
24 And he cried and said, Father Abraham, have mercy on me, and send Lazarus, that he may dip the tip of his finger in water, and cool my tongue; for I am tormented in this flame.
25 But Abraham said, Son, remember that thou in thy lifetime receivedst thy good things, and likewise

Lazarus evil things: but now he is comforted, and thou art tormented.

26 And beside all this, between us and you there is a great gulf fixed: so that they which would pass from hence to you cannot; neither can they pass to us, that would come from thence.

27 Then he said, I pray thee therefore, father, that thou wouldest send him to my father's house:

28 For I have five brethren; that he may testify unto them, lest they also come into this place of torment.

29 Abraham saith unto him, They have Moses and the prophets; let them hear them.

30 And he said, Nay, father Abraham: but if one went unto them from the dead, they will repent.

31 And he said unto him, If they hear not Moses and the prophets, neither will they be persuaded, though one rose from the dead.

For those who believe there is a God, if you will go into the Bible, you'll find this portion of Scripture is written in red. The red letters show us these are the Words spoken by Jesus Christ; the only Son of God, (Who by the way, was later raised from the dead).

Yet you still have trouble believing His Words?

"One day I pray that the United States of America would repent and come to the knowledge of our Lord and Savior Jesus Christ like they do in Honduras."

4 Faces of Death

The Main purpose of our trips to this country:

- **1.** We allow God to work in our lives through the personal enrichment that comes from this type of mission trip.
- **2.** We are saturated in the heart of the ministry as we cover several churches each evening. The things that happen there are incredible as God reaches out to the people that He loves with demonstrations that go beyond description. We hold crusades, conferences on worship, and speak to the leaders of the nation.
- **3.** We work side by side with teams of ministers to bring them food and medical supplies as we travel throughout the country in small villages as well as large cities.

Chapter 5

The 2nd Face of Death
A Man was Killed on the Highway

The following week after this first man's death, our whole team seemed to have been energized with zeal to tell people about how powerful our God really was. It was taking most of us an incredible amount of time just to digest what was happening already on this incredible journey God had put us on.

And then it happened again, without any warning we found ourselves being enveloped into the scene as yet, another man being killed on the highway just in front of us. Once again this took place on a Monday and once again we were returning from the beach from our day of rest.

We were on a four lane highway coming back from the city of La Lima Cortes: just 10 miles west of San Pedro Sula. The crowed had already started forming on both sides of this major highway—to witness the gruesome scene.

Have you ever wondered why so many people want to stop and see something like this? The majority of us are infatuated with a horrible accident death throws at us. Yet at the same time, (in disbelief) we are scared of the reality that confronts us when we witness it.

The rescue team of fireman, EMTs and the news media from Channel 6 were already there and had taken a fallen tree and placed it in the highway as a barrier to stop the traffic from running over them. When we pulled the bus over on the side of the road our team quickly ran over to the man lying on the road [expecting] to see God raise this one from the dead like He had done the week before.

I'm only sharing the details of what happened not because I'm morbid, but only as an eye witness to this tragic event. So please forgive me, and bear with me while I try my best to describe this story in hopes you (the reader) can see the hand of God's mercy reaching out to this family while in their distress.

As I got off the bus, I heard these words come up out of my spirit, *"I'm not going to raise this one up."* Just behind the bus I saw the handlebars of a bicycle with a man's hand and forearm still attached to it. Apparently the man was heading in the direction leading away from the city as he rode his bike. Someone hit him from behind and threw him across the media where he was struck again from oncoming traffic.

His wife was standing next to him: in a state of shock. Jim Coleman, one of our ministers was consoling her and when he touched her she fell under the power of God into the street next to her husband's body. The rescue team immediately came to assist her and Jim told them she was okay and that God had touched her in that moment. They then turned and walked away from her... *hum, interesting?*

～

As I got off the bus, I heard these words come up out of my spirit, *"I'm not going to raise this one up."*

Joe, our fireman from New Orleans was on his knees next to the man praying for him. He looked up at me and asked, *"Will God do it again?"* I knew at that moment, He was not going to raise this one up—as I shook my head no.

Mauricio our bus driver had pulled some Gospel tracks off the bus and was passing them out to the crowds of people standing in the street. He had prayed for many to receive Jesus into their heart.

Then out of this crowd came a woman named Rosa speaking (in English) saying, *"I know that God is going to do something great here."* I found out later, the man who had been hit was her brother-in-law.

I was standing no more than four feet away from this man's body and every so often you would see blood start pumping out of the man's torn arm. I was total consumed with the scene that was presented in front of me. Then a gentleman from the TV station walked up to me and asked me a question that completely caught me off guard.

He said, *"There is a Christian radio station up in the mountains. They have an all-day marathon going on the next day to raise up money to help keep them on the air for another year."* He also told me, the man who owned the TV channel in San Pedro Sula was an atheist but had agreed to allow them to use his facilities for 24 hours at no cost. He then invited our worship team to come to the station to play live on the air.

I agreed to come, and the rest of what happened at the scene was like a blur to me as we got back on the bus and headed back to our home base. I do remember how odd it felt with this invitation taking place right next to the dead man on the road.

Once again there was not much talking going on in the bus. But what was waiting for us the next day would begin to unravel the mystery of what took place before us on that day.

The air was filled with confusion that morning as we gathered around the room for our daily devotions. The question that stood out the most (to all of us) was why God had not raised this second man from the dead? So now our great zeal had been replaced with a sense of confusion and the question–what happens now?

Chapter 6

The Rest of the Story

If you remember in the case of the first death we encountered, two of our team members both said they heard God say to grab the man by his toes. Even though that sounds weird; in this case, one obeyed and the other didn't. But the moment Shawn obeyed—the man set right up healed and rose from the dead.

I asked the group in our meeting that morning, if anyone had heard God say that He would raise up this second man like He had done with the first man. I then told them what He said to me about not raising him up. Now I understand you may be having a problem with me saying God spoke to me. So here are some Scriptures that I believe support what I'm sharing here.

If you remember earlier in this book I said I take it seriously that the Word of God is the source of my faith and I do not apologize for using it in my defense.

So then faith comes by hearing ...the word [Rhema] of God" (Ro 10:17). If you cannot hear the Word of God when it is spoken to you then how will you ever have faith? Could a just God require you to have faith and then be a God Who is unable to speak to you anymore? Our Father in Heaven is not a dumb idol like many 'gods' that we see throughout the earth. He is very capable of speaking to us when the time arises. When God speaks to us He does not respond to us because of some religious form or formula.

In the *Gospel of John chapter nine,* we see Jesus healing a blind man by mixing dust, spitting on it, forming mud and then applying it to the blind man's eyes. Then He sent this man to the pool of Siloam to wash the mud out of his eyes and he was miraculously healed.

A friend of mine out of Illinois (I won't mention his name here) tried this on an inmate at a prison once and was kicked out of the prison ministry for it. If he heard God tell him to do this (as He told Jesus) then the blind would have been healed. No formula will cause God to heal someone for you. Faith comes by hearing God's Voice and then obeying (or taking action) in response to what God said for you to do.

Just a thought here: you will never heal anyone by your own desire to; God is the healer–not you. Jesus healed the blind with other means, but for time's sake you can go to the Bible and read for yourself about them. These are found in *(Mt 9:29; Mr 10:52).*

What was Jesus' secret for His ministry? I submit to you that He had a proper relationship with His heavenly Father. Jesus said, *"I do always those things that please the Father"*

4 Faces of Death

(John 8:29). Because the condition of Jesus' heart was always right (can this be said about you always? A hard heart can keep you from hearing His Voice) with His heavenly Father, He could easily hear and obey His Father's Voice.

Jesus made it clear, *"The Son can do nothing by himself. He does only what he sees the Father doing, and in the same way he sees the Father doing it" (Jo 5:19 TLB).*

One more passage of Scripture I would like to say here in my defense on hearing God's Voice: it is found in *John 10*.

> *John 10:27-30 NKJV*
> *27 My sheep hear My voice, and I know them, and they follow Me.*
> *28 And I give them eternal life, and they shall never perish; neither shall anyone snatch them out of My hand.*
> *29 My Father, who has given them to Me, is greater than all; and no one is able to snatch them out of My Father's hand.*
> *30 I and My Father are one."*

~

When God speaks to us He does not respond to us because of some religious form or formula.

For you who don't believe there is a God, of course then

all of this makes no sense to you in anyway. But for all of those who have called on the Name of Jesus and received Him into their hearts, you are now His sheep and you have a right as a child of God to hear the Voice of God.

So let's return back to the devotions that morning. Because we had an appointment at the TV station, our meeting had to be shortened. Not only the TV, but also we were to be at the Pastors Association in the city that morning as well—it was going to be a busy day.

When we arrived at the TV station Mike and the rest of the team began to set up our equipment for the program. The News commentator who had invited us to this place came up and asked me if I had known the man on the highway. I told him that I had never met him and he then began to tell me an amazing story about the guy.

He said he had known him for a long time and that he was one of the nicest people you could have ever met. He said he would give you the shirt off of his back; and then walk miles just to give it to you.

Just a few days earlier he had come to his office and told him he had this terrible feeling that he was going to die. The gentleman from the station asked his friend if he had ever made Jesus the Lord of his life and he replied, *"No not yet."* Then he told him he needed to do this right away, so they prayed and the man received Jesus into his heart; the accident happened two days later—taking his life. Praise God for His mercy and the obedience of a friend.

We had finished our appointment there and then headed to the Pastors Association for the morning's meeting that was held every Tuesday. When we arrived there you could feel tension in the air as the pastors were trying to decide on whether to participate in the marathon that day or not.

We told them we had just returned from there and that it was a good opportunity to reach out to the lost: with it being a secular station and all. So everyone settled down to have the morning meeting and many of them decided to go and set in on the program.

I'm standing in the back of the church when Rosa (the sister-in-law of the second man killed on the highway) came up to me in tears. You have to understand, this is a city of three or four hundred thousand people and is the third largest city in the country and she finds me at this meeting. I'm moved by her anguish as she starts sharing with me her part of this story.

Do you remember me sharing with you how she believed God was going to do something great here today? Now she is explaining to me how she had tried to witness to him many times but he would not accept Jesus into his heart. Through tears she said to me, *"I am tormented in my soul because I know he has gone to Hell. I could not even go to the wake because of this pain in my heart for him."*

I was able to give her a peace of mind when I shared with her about what happened that morning and the testimony I had received of him being saved just two days earlier. She was so happy, she began to shout and laugh; and the tears that were flowing down her cheeks were now tears of pure joy, Amen!

~

Praise God for His mercy and the obedience of a friend.

She then told me that she was at a meeting in one of the soccer stadiums the night before his death and someone approached her saying, she needed to be strong in her faith because something bad was going to happen.

I had felt in my heart I was supposed to go to that meeting but we had no transportation. I will never know what might have happened if I could have gone there but it played a major part in me looking into bringing a bus to Honduras so that transportation would never be an issue again. I thought this was the end of this story but there is still more to come.

There are two more stories with the face of death on them, but I need to move forward a little bit to share with you more of the story about this second face of death.

We were at the airport getting ready for our return flight

to the USA. The woman behind the counter was very nice and placed her hands on my hand thanking me for our service to their country. I thought she was thanking me for not getting upset with her when she told me I had too much weight in my baggage. I just made the adjustments and away I went to go through customs.

["*I am ashamed to have to say this but some of the rudest people I have seen over the years in the airports are preachers demanding their rights with the attendants at the counter. It made me almost ashamed to mention to them that I am a minister as well.*

"Anyway that's enough with one of my pet peeves."]

As we were making our way upstairs to go through the scanners, Danny (my older brother) came up to me and asked me if the woman at the counter had said anything to me. I told him what had happened and he said that she was thanking us for loving her country and was grateful for what we did to help the family of the man killed on the highway. She knew him well because he worked in the back of the airport in luggage. It is a small world isn't it?

This story gets even better in time, but for now I want to continue with the events of this trip by sharing the testimony of the third face of death. When I finish up the last chapter of this book I will share some more details about Rosa and some other people who fit into the mix.

4 Faces of Death

"Honduras is a nation desperately needing to hear the good news of Jesus Christ."

4 Faces of Death

Chapter 7

The 3rd Face of Death
A Man Dies from Fear

This chapter might get a little complicated to communicate with you all of the details concerning the circumstances that happened before and after His death. So bear with me for the moment as I attempt to put it down on paper so you can understand the sequence of events leading up to, and through to the end of this man's story.

While we continued on our adventure called, the '4 Faces of Death' we received a call from a pastor friend of Mauricio's who lived up in the mountains in a town called; Ocotepeque. This town was *nestled down in a valley surrounded by some of the largest mountains found in western Honduras.
*SOURCE: Freedom from the Fear of Death (on the web)

The man who called him was a pastor of a church there, and his son had been robbed at gunpoint and was visibly shaken by the confrontation. Fear had run its course and was now tormenting his son [beyond] just having a normal reaction from fear. He was requesting some Scriptures he could share with his son that would help bring him some relief. So we sent him Scriptures like these to help bring comfort to his dilemma.

45

4 Faces of Death

For God hath not given us the spirit of fear; but of power, and of love, and of a sound mind.

Philippians 4:6-7
Be careful for nothing; but in everything by prayer and supplication with thanksgiving let your requests be made known unto God.

1 John 4:18
There is no fear in love; but perfect love casteth out fear: because fear hath torment. He that feareth is not made perfect in love.

Romans 8:26
Likewise the Spirit also helpeth our infirmities: for we know not what we should pray for as we ought: but the Spirit itself maketh intercession for us with groanings which cannot be uttered.

2 Timothy 1:6-7
Wherefore I put thee in remembrance that thou stir up the gift of God, which is in thee by the putting on of my hands

Romans 8:15
For ye have not received the spirit of bondage again to fear; but ye have received the Spirit of adoption, whereby we cry, Abba, Father.

4 Faces of Death

Hebrews 13:6
So that we may boldly say, The Lord [is] my helper,
and I will not fear what man shall do unto me.

The fear was so great on this young man that two days later–he died from that fear. I told Mauricio lets go up into the mountains and pray for his family. He was all for it until I mentioned that I also wanted to pray for the man that had died. He said, *"but he's dead!"* and I replied, *"Yes but so was the first man on the highway."* He would not take me up there, which is reason number two for us getting our own bus.

∾

For God hath not given us the spirit of fear; but of power, and of love, and of a sound mind.

I thought this would be the end of this story–but boy was I wrong. God had some unfinished business with this third man, and I was soon going to be thrown back into this testimony once again.

So in order to continue with this story I need to move forward before sharing the fourth face of death that we encountered there on this trip. So here we go!

It was eight months later after I returned back to Tulsa, Oklahoma as we were preparing for our next visit to Honduras; I was setting in my office praying. For the sake of not having to explain myself I will say that I had a dream (although I was wide awake and some people would call it a vision). But I had a dream that I was on a bus and we were climbing up a mountain. It was high and beautiful, and one of the most awesome sights a man can lay his eyes on.

Half way up the mountain we ran into a horrible storm, the clouds were dark and lightning was flashing all around us. Then as we came to the top of the mountain, we broke through the storm. You could look down and see the storm clouds and lightning striking the mountain below. But on top of the mountain you could see for miles and miles. It was breathtaking to see and I remember in the dream how I wanted to go to this place and visit there. Then as quickly as the dream started—it was gone. I found myself praying over this beautiful place and wondered why I had seen it in this dream that was so vivid.

Two months later we arrived back in San Pedro Sula and headed for our old familiar refuge at the Youth for Christ Ministries. Mauricio had set up our schedule for us, since most places had Spanish names; I really tried not to make it my business to worry about where we were going.

We went to a town called, *La Entrada.* The name of this city means 'The Entrance' and it was at the entrance to the State of Copan. There is a famous place of sacrifice (where Mayan ruins are), that seems to attract a lot of people to come to see it: thousands of people have been murdered there to their gods. I'm not sure why anyone would want to go and see this horrible place. There was a lot of witch-craft there and we were setting up a crusade in the local town square that night.

The people came by the hundreds to see what these gringos had to say. The local police asked us to pray just before our meeting started because a man was going through the city murdering and had killed five people already that night. During the meeting, there had been a car accident just on the main highway that had claimed the lives of four more people. So there were nine people who had already lost their lives during that first night of our meeting in that city.

When we had the alter call no one came forward for prayer. They all stood around the edge of the park like they were afraid to move. A tall man with a stick started to move for-ward and was saying things that I could not understand. The language he was speaking was not Spanish and you could tell by the tone of his voice—it wasn't friendly either.

My older brother Danny was speaking from the platform at the time and began to speak the Name of Jesus over the situation. Every time he mentioned Jesus' Name the man would fall backwards. Danny keeps repeating the Name of Jesus over and over until the man turned and ran out of the meeting—screaming as he went.

4 Faces of Death

Mauricio had brought several teenagers who could speak perfect English and while Danny preached from the platform we took several of these teens to the people and we prayed for hundreds of them to receive Jesus into their hearts that night. The spirit of darkness and death had been broken that night. Praise God!

The next day we were packed up and ready to go to our next location which was up on this high mountain. I was setting in the front seat of the bus with a Honduran who was from the church that we were going to; with his broken English and my broken Spanish we were able to communicate with each other.

I found out he was the brother of the man that had died from the spirit of fear. I could not believe this was actually happening. His father was the pastor of the church that we were going to be ministering in that night. While climbing the mountain we went into a storm with dark clouds and lightning striking all around our bus (just like in the vision [dream] I had in my office two months earlier), we burst through the dark clouds into one of the most beautiful breathtaking scenes I have ever laid my eyes on.

There in the valley of these huge mountains was our destiny; Ocotepeque. The Lord spoke to me and said there were multitudes in the valley of decision. My heart was pumping wildly in my chest with just the thought that God would actually bring me to a place like this. Soon I would come to know what God had in mind for us that goes beyond anything I could have ever imagined.

When we arrived at the church we were so busy setting up the equipment for the meeting that I never got to meet the pastor personally. Mauricio gave us instructions on what the pastor wanted for the service. Once ready for the meeting we were praying for the service and the Lord showed me a vision of Him standing with one foot on one mountain and another foot on another mountain. He had His hand stretched over this city.

Then he spoke to me these words, *"You think that you came here just to do a service, but I tell you that I brought you here. These are the multitudes I spoke to you about who are in the valley of decision."* I began to weep for the souls of the people that were crowded into this church. The people responded in expectation of receiving what they came for.

God had manifested his presence in such a magnificent way: healings, deliverances, hundreds of Salvations, and much more were falling on the men, women and children who were in attendance there that night. When the meeting was over the pastor begged us to stay there for the night but we had two people who were flying out in the morning that needed to get to the airport.

At two o'clock in the morning coming down out of the mountains we were pulled over by three banditos that had

4 Faces of Death

masks on and were carrying AK-47s. One man boarded our bus walking from the front to the back never saying a word. We were all speechless and praying under our breath. This man had hit the jackpot because we all had our passports, as well as, all of our money and equipment. He walked back towards the bus driver and growled at him motioning us to go.

I don't know what that man saw on our bus that night; maybe he saw peasants or maybe the Lord didn't allow him to see any of us on the bus. But for whatever reason– we drove away unharmed.

My last comment about this testimony happened after we arrived back in Tulsa Ok. I was on death row getting ready for our weekly service when one of the inmates came up to me asking me where in the world was I on such and such night at 2:00 in the morning. He said God woke him up and showed him my face and he started praying for me until he got peace about it. It was exactly the same day and the same time we were being pulled over in Honduras.

Amazing that some people would say, there is no God; my question to you is: if there is no God, then what happened in this exchange of encounters that were done hundreds and hundreds of miles apart. Okay, I am convinced (there is a God), so I don't have a problem with him reaching into my life and rescuing me. But I hope by now you may be softening to the fact that there is someone out there Who is much bigger then you, and He has you on His mind.

4 Faces of Death

I am sure by now, many people have picked up this book and some have judged me as a lunatic, and have discarded it into the trash can. Well so be it! But I am convinced that many of you are still hanging onto this book as the Spirit of God is drawing you to join Him in His Kingdom. Your soul is weighing in the balance and I'm praying that you will see things for what they really are and come to Him before it is too late.

～

"These are the multitudes I spoke to you about who are in the valley of decision."

Here is some interesting information I found on the internet that describes what the valley of decision might be.

I have some added information that will be presented to you at the end of this book. Testimony's from Rosa, Alex, Nick, and a few others who have tasted death and can tell you their side of the story of more faces of death then the four mentioned in this book.

So with that, I have one more face of death we dealt with on this mission trip (which started me writing on this book).

4 Faces of Death

And when he thus had spoken,
he cried with a loud voice, Lazarus, come forth.
And he that was dead came forth,
bound hand and foot with graveclothes:
and his face was bound about with a napkin.
Jesus saith unto them,
Loose him, and let him go.
John 11:43-44

4 Faces of Death

Chapter 8

The 4th Face of Death
My Brother Danny

While the time of our departure was drawing near for us to return back to our cities and states. We still had one more testimony that needed to be added to our unbelievable encounters with these first three faces of death. I was growing incredibly tired from all of the meetings that we had held all across the country of Honduras. I was not counting these events in order to write a book, but these events were happening for me to take the initiative to write them down for you (the reader) to consider what happens to you after you've been faced with the issue of death. I believe you now have the opportunity to change your destiny while you are still here on planet earth.

As I lay down on my bed the night before heading home I kept waking up rebuking a spirt of death that seemed to be hanging over our group. I don't recall how many times I had woke up speaking to this unwanted visitor of death to go in the Name of Jesus; but it was quite a few times.

At breakfast Danny and I were talking and he told me that he kept waking up all night long thinking he was going to die. I asked the Lord why Danny was feeling this way and why had he awakened both of us out of our sleep multiple times to address this issue of death.

I believe there are many people every day who are struggling with this issue of death, both within The Church, as well as those who are outside of The Church. And we as people of God who have already made our decisions to follow Jesus have a responsibility to reach out to those around us who have been running away in fear of what awaits them when death comes knocking at their door.

~

I believe you now have the opportunity to change your destiny while you are still here on planet earth.

I've had plenty of time to rehearse the situations I have presented to you in this book. Yet I feel like I have missed something that would convince you there is really a God out there Who wants to rescue you from the grips of the devil. Somebody once said that he didn't believe in the devil, and the devil quickly replied—neither do I.

There have been many testimonies of those who have crossed over to the other side and saw the realities of Heaven and Hell and were brought back here to testify about it.

4 Faces of Death

A Doctor Told Me...

As told by a State Prison Chaplain

A good friend of mine who was a chaplain at one of the prisons here in Oklahoma shared this testimony with me many years ago. He had a good friend who was a doctor in a hospital, he worked in the emergency room and his job was to use the Defibrillator in life-threatening situations. He told Jack that in the course of a year he had seven patients who had died in the emergency room and he revived them.

Listen to what he said next! In all seven patients that he used the defibrillator on: once there heart started working again they all said the same thing to him. They described what Hell was like (and each description was exactly the same [from all seven] patients).

This doctor told Jack he was a believer but that he was completely wrapped up in his job with not much time devoted to his Christianity and his love for Jesus. This had opened up his eyes to the fact that he needed to recommit his life to Christ.

Then he said four out of the seven that got saved, still to this day remember great details about their experience while in Hell. The other three said they didn't see anything and that everything was just black.

▶ 1. So let me ask you this question: is Hell a real place?

▶ **2.** And if there really is a Hell, is there a way of escape from its death grip

▶ **3.** Why would a God Who loves us send people there?

Jesus talked about Hell more than He talked about Heaven. Most Christians refuse to acknowledge there is such a place. Eternal death means to be totally separated from God; we were created to live forever. If you reject God and His Son Jesus Christ then you will live forever in this place that was not created for you; but it was created for the devil and those that follow him.

If you receive Jesus Christ into your heart and you have been born-again, you will live forever in Heaven which is surrounded by His presence; and I can tell you, that it is a much better place to be.

[Here's another amazing testimony:]

Jesus Showed Me Paradise

Written by Jerrie Childers

Jerrie Childers lives in the city of Broken Arrow, OK. The following is quoted from her letter to me about her near death experience.

She said, "It was in July of 1969. I was 16 years old and was also around four and a half months pregnant. We were at my husbands grandmother's house, and all day long I had an inner knowing something big was going to happen when the astronauts touched down on the moon.

We went to bed that night and I was fine, but by the next morning when we woke up–I was very sick; I had a high fever and was confused. George called my mom and together they took me to the Dr. I was then admitted into the hospital; they diagnosed me with double pneumonia and severe pneumonia.

The doctor didn't think I would even make it through the night. Someone said there was a girl across the hall from me that had the very same diagnosis. I was so weak I couldn't even raise my arms up to feed myself. Because I was so sick they had to put me in isolation so I wouldn't be exposed to any other diseases.

While lying in the bed I heard a knocking at the door. I said, *"Open the door and let them in."* No one was at the door. A little later I again heard a knocking at the door, and again I said, *"Open the door and let them in."* And again they said there was no one at the door. The third time that I heard a knocking at the door I was aware of angels at the head of my bed on each side of me.

They said it is the Lord knocking at your heart's door. I said, *"Yes Lord."* He took me with Him and showed me the most beautiful Paradise with brilliant vibrant colors. He said I could stay, or I could go back if I wanted to. I said, *"Lord I want to have my baby and be with my baby."*

4 Faces of Death

He took me back. When I woke up I was surrounded by nurses and Doctors.

I grew stronger throughout the day. The next morning I was strong enough and had gotten out of bed, dressed myself and was setting up in a chair when everyone came into my room. They were all amazed (considering the day before I couldn't even raise my arms up at all). Someone said the girl across the hall had passed away during the night.

Jerrie had made a decision to accept Jesus into her heart before having this near death experience, and her place to reside after death, will be this wonderful, and beautiful Paradise.

No Vital Signs at All!

Written by Aaron Jones

My wife Anita teaches at a private school in Tulsa, Oklahoma. Several years ago, my brother and I were selling printing to businesses door to door in Sapulpa (a suburb of Tulsa), when I received a call on my cell phone. It was my wife's boss, she said in a very anxious tone: *"Anita is having some sort of spell or attack, we have called an ambulance; you need to get here as quickly as you can."*

I knew immediately, it was an Asthma attack (since she had some trouble with it in the past), I just didn't realize at the time how serious. We both jumped in my truck and headed for Tulsa. On the way my cell phone rang again, and once again it was her boss; only this time she was crying and in a panic, almost screaming in my ear, *"It's bad Aaron, go straight to the hospital. We will meet you there, the paramedics are working on her—they don't know if she is going to make it! ...it's bad, IT'S BAD!"*

Now I am driving my SUV at near 100 mph up 66 Hwy with flashers on headed for the hospital. The devil was in my ear the entire time saying, *"She's dead, you know she's already gone! You're going to have to raise your children by yourself. You won't have a wife, you'll be single and alone. It's over, Anita is dead and you're going to have to start all over again. What are you going to tell your daughters?"* When I would rebuke 'the spirit of death', he would say, *"That doesn't work, she's already gone! She's dead, your wife is dead!"* I think the enemy said it a hundred times between Sapulpa and Tulsa; he would not shut up.

When we arrived at the Emergency Room, the ambulance had not got there yet, then to make it appear even worse (the devil does that to intimidate and cause fear) when the ambulance did finally turn the corner they came in slowly with no emergency lights running. I have to admit—it did [look] BAD!

When a male paramedic opened the back doors of the ambulance, there was a female paramedic on top of my wife beating on Anita's chest trying to get her to breathe.

4 Faces of Death

The two male paramedics lowered the gurney to the concrete, all the while the one by her head was squeezing a manual respirator (bagging her) as the female paramedic frantically kept trying to get her to breathe on her own.

Anita's blouse and bra had been cut and stripped away, but from only a few feet away you almost couldn't tell it. Have you ever seen these modern day Body Paint models (they really aren't wearing enough clothing, but it looks like they are)? The illusion is caused by painting their skin with bright colors. From the waist all the way up to just under her eyes, my wife was as blue as the blue jeans she was wearing; to me it seemed, her neck, chest and hands looked like she was a 'Smurf'. It sounds funny now, but at that moment it was terrifying. Also, her mouth and eyes were wide open, and her eyes were glazed over and never blinked (they were locked in a dead stare).

Keep in mind that although to me, it seemed like eternity: all this actually happened from the back of the ambulance to just inside the Emergency Room doors—in only seconds.

I told one of the paramedics she was my wife and I was a Minister and I needed to pray for her, now! He responded, *"You do whatever you need to do, because we are getting NO VITAL SIGNS AT ALL!"*

I placed one hand on her arm and one on her [ice cold]

forehead as we ran with the gurney into the Emergency Room. I was praying everything I knew to say, when suddenly I shouted very loud, *"You look at me Anita! LOOK AT ME! YOU LIVE IN JESUS' NAME!"* At that moment she blinked her eyes, turned her head and looked directly at me. The female paramedic screamed, *"She just looked at him!"* I said, *"She's going to make it,"* as I started crying; then a doctor (or someone in a white coat) shoved me out the doors saying, I'd have to wait outside.

I called two of my ministry board members, a missionary friend and my Pastor, I told them, *"Anita died from some sort of attack—PRAY!"*

Then I began to talk to God, I remember almost every word, *"Lord you know me, I need my wife. If this is selfish I'm sorry, but you know I am too stupid to raise two daughters by myself. And another woman to be their mom is not going to work, so I need You to do something Father; I NEED YOUR HELP!"*

Within what seemed like minutes, a nurse came out in the parking garage and asked if I was Mr. Jones, she then told me I could see my wife. I asked, *"What happened, is she okay?"* Walking away from me she raised her hands and kind'a shrugged her shoulders as if to signify she didn't have a clue, as she answered, *"I don't know what happened, you are just going to have to talk to the doctor."*

4 Faces of Death

When I walked into her hospital room, Anita was sitting in the bed looking around like she didn't know where she was. I asked her if she was alright, but she didn't answer; her eyes were as big as silver dollars, and she seemed confused. I asked her if she knew me, but again, she didn't answer—she only looked at me.

By the time a doctor came in, my mom and oldest daughter had also arrived and were with us in the room. I asked the doctor, *"Is she okay?"* The doctor replied, *"I don't know, we don't know what happened? We think it was an acute Asthma attack coupled with an allergic reaction to something in her classroom? We do know, that one minute she was in trouble and the next minute she wasn't in any trouble at all."*

I hesitantly asked, *"Was she dead?"* The doctor answered, *"Well, where she went most people don't come back from."* She turned to my wife and said, *"You are one lucky girl. We're going to take you back in a minute and make sure you don't have any brain issues from loss of oxygen."*

I told her, *"I'm a minister and I had several people praying for her."* She attempted to shrug that statement off, saying, *"That might have been it."* But I said, *"No, that is it! You already said, you didn't know what happened. Why count prayer and God out of the deal?"* She smiled and said, *"Well, someone up there was sure watching out for you."*

4 Faces of Death

They came back from the tests with even more [proof] God had intervened in this situation. The doctor sounded as if she almost questioned the results, saying, *"Usually when there has been this kind of episode there is evidence of it in a person's blood. But we can't even tell she ever had a problem; it's just one of those things we can't answer. Glad she is okay, I guess we are going to let her go home."*

While we waited for her mom to bring her more clothes and for the check-out paperwork to be completed, two of the paramedics from the ambulance stopped in to see the MIRACLE that was evidently already being talked about among the hospital staff. They were both amazed she was sitting there talking to everyone and going home. They said they hadn't seen too many good endings to such an ordeal, and told us they were very happy for us.

Then as we left the hospital, just like the Bible story of Jesus raising the little girl from the dead, my wife said, *"I'm hungry."* So I took her to one of our favorite local BBQ restaurants. At the table I asked the waitress for a knife or scissors to cut the hospital bracelet off of Anita's wrist. The waitress put her hand on my wife's shoulder and asked, *"Oh honey were you sick?"* I told her, *"Hey, about two hours ago she was dead!"* She quickly pulled her hand away as she turned a little pale and went to get the scissors. Ha!

God is bound to have an incredible sense of humor. Isn't

4 Faces of Death

He amazing? We serve an AWESOME GOD!

Anita said later, that she had not seen anything or heard anything when she went over on the other side; only that it was all peace, a peace like she had never experienced here. She said it was so perfect a peace, that even though she loved me and our daughters there was no desire to come back and leave that peace.

Snatched From the Clutches of Death
The following account is an excerpt from
'C.H.P. - Coffee Has Priority'
(The Memoirs of a California Highway Patrol Officer Badge 9045)
Written by Ed Marr ▪ Used by permission.

I looked skyward enjoying the warm, balmy breeze of the evening, taking in the smell of fresh air. Knowing it was nearing the end of my shift and three days off, I proceeded back to the barn to close out my eleventh consecutive work day, hoping that somewhere and some how South San Diego County would remain quiet as it had been throughout the day. I prayed to God that I could make it back to my area office without incident, when suddenly radio dispatch called me saying, 87-5. San Diego! I picked up the mike and answered, San Diego, 87-5, northbound I-5 approaching National City, go ahead! Dispatch: There's an (11-79) major injury, possible fatality collision northbound I-5 south of the Coronado Bay Bridge. I responded code 3 and within minutes I arrived first, being the closest unit. Notifying dispatch as being

4 Faces of Death

(10-97) at the scene, I quickly secured the collision scene within the north bound lanes of I-5 and requested additional assistance (tow trucks, coroner, paramedics and additional CHP units). Making a quick mental assessment of the scene, I went about creating my flare pattern from the rear (south bound) side of the collision scene, so as to forewarn on coming northbound traffic.

Some good Samaritans did stop along the shoulder of I-5 near the scene and ran out towards me offering their help. Now typically under normal conditions, such help would be refused however, given the precarious location of this collision in a darkened stretch of freeway and in a blind curve to approaching northbound vehicles, I accepted their assistance. In short order, additional units had arrived to maintain the rear guard and to protect those of us at the scene from approaching northbound traffic. At this time, I was able to further assess the scene. In the northbound number 2 and 3 traffic lanes, I saw Vehicle One (V-1). It was a green 1974 Mercury Monarch, on its wheels basically facing north. It had sustained massive rear end collision damage. I noticed Vehicle Two (V-2). It was a blue 1967 Mercury Montego that basically faced north and it was positioned on the unimproved right shoulder of I-5 at or near the collision scene. V-2 had sustained massive front end collision damage. The driver, an older man, was found seated in the left front seat of V-2 obviously expired. He had been impaled through the chest on the steering column and his upper body was positioned in and through the windshield.

Redirecting my attention to V-1, I walked around its right side in the darkness following the beam of my flashlight. I noticed a heavy red liquid on the pavement streaming from beneath V-1. Suspecting it to be transmission fluid, I walked on until I discovered to my horror the lower extremities of a person underneath V-1. I trained my flashlight on this person, and realized that this person seemed to be a woman and the liquid was not transmission fluid at all, but a copious amount of fatal blood! This person was face down on the pavement with nearly two tons of V-1 on top of her! As she laid there, her body twitched (in the throws of death) and the sight and smell of her demise was evident! I instructed the good Samaritans to assist me flipping V-1 onto its right side, being careful not to slip in the large pool of blood. Having accomplished this, we all noticed that this person was in fact a young woman. She lay there on the pavement slowly loosing her life; (after all, life is in the blood).

Let me describe her injuries. As I said, this woman was found beneath V-1. Through the course of my investigation and the evidence available, it was obvious that she either was knocked down or thrown to the pavement upon impact with V-2, which caused V-1 to crash down on top of her little body. Her upper torso had been completely crushed as though she had been die-stamped into a mold with extreme weight of pressure! I mean, her entire upper half was completely flattened! From her head to her waist, she was as flat as my citation book! As for her head, her skin served as a bag wherein her skull fragments, brain, sinuses, eyes, etc. were contained! Standing by, all we could do was take note of her faint groans and watch this poor woman expire as we waited for the paramedics to arrive. Thanking these good Samaritans for their assistance, I instructed them to leave the area. In the meantime, I proceeded to complete my scene investigation. Through the scene evidence, I learned that this woman apparently was looking under the hood of V-1 after it had broken down in the northbound number 3 traffic lane. It was at this time that northbound V-2 plowed into the rear of V-1 at full freeway speed (65-70mph). This impact forced V-1 forward, swallowing this woman under the hood. She was spit out onto the pavement after having traveled several feet forward inside V-1's engine compartment. The evidence revealed that V-1 spun about vertically on its front bumper and then crashed down on top of this woman, who was now a pedestrian.

The paramedics did arrive shortly after I released the good Samaritans. One of the paramedics approached me and requested that I drive the ambulance to the nearest hospital. I obeyed his request and informed the other CHP officers at the scene as well as radio dispatch of this. The paramedic stated, Believe it or not officer, we've got a faint pulse!

4 Faces of Death

So here I am, driving this meat wagon to Balboa Naval Hospital. Talk about bells and whistles! This vehicle had it all. So I flipped every switch on its instrument board I saw as I departed. Good thing it wasn't a computer! With all the switches I flipped, had this ambulance been a computer, we probably would have all been deleted from off the face of the earth! We had about a 10 minute drive before we arrived at the Hospital. I allowed my thoughts to wonder about my life as memories flashed through the vast theater of my mind.

The Hospital entrance was in sight. Turning left from Pershing Drive, I proceeded up the hill towards the Emergency entrance, where a team of medics waited for our arrival. I pulled under the overhead and stopped. Immediately, the paramedics and the medical staff removed this young woman from the ambulance and wheeled her into the ER. I followed. As the medical team attempted to sustain her life, I stood at the foot of her bed and prayed over her broken body that Almighty God would repair this young woman's life and livelihood.

Thinking nothing more about her, I departed. I notified my radio dispatch that I was ready to be picked up at the Hospital for transport back to my patrol vehicle, which I had parked at the collision scene. I drove my vehicle back to the barn, completed my paperwork and secured for the night. I had two days off. Upon my return to work, I found a note in my office mail box (pigeon hole). The

4 Faces of Death

note instructed me that I was to call Doctor So and So at the Balboa Naval Hospital at my earliest convenience.

I called the good doctor and this is the gist of his conversation. Officer Marr? Yes sir! I am so glad you returned my call! I said, Doctor, Do you have something to tell me? Officer, I certainly do! Of course you remember the young college student that you brought in two days ago with the severe head and torso trauma? Yes sir, I remember. Well Officer, are you standing up or are you sitting down? I said, Doc! Just tell me what's going on! He said, Okay then. Officer Marr! Several of my team saw you standing at the foot of her bed praying. I said, do you have a problem with this Doctor? The doctor said, Hold on Officer Marr, please hear me out! You left and in your absence certain things occurred, which I thought should be brought to your attention. The Doctor went on to say, Officer Marr! I don't know what you said or what you did, but know this. What I am about to tell you, every member of my team wants you to know that a miracle took place right before our very eyes! I said, Doc! Tell me what happened! He said, you left and while the six of us where attempting to stabilize this woman, skull fragments began to pop back in place! Then her soft tissues within her skull were seemingly recreated before our eyes! Officer Marr! This woman was released this morning! She walked out of here under own power! What ever you said or did Officer Marr, all of us here at the hospital want you to know that we saw a miracle take place! Keep up the good work, Officer Marr!

4 Faces of Death

The Testimony of a Friend
Written by Wayne Sanders

I am setting here in my office going over the events that took place in the early part of March of 2017. A very good friend of mine shared some things with me while in the hospital but preferred to remain anonymous. He suffered a heart attack and flat lined several times and the experience that he shared with me I felt was remarkable; and with his permission, I feel compelled to share this testimony with you.

I will do my best to explain the details that I know about this situation with you on what he had personally experienced just as he shared them with me. The reason for gathering this kind of information is to bring to light that there is life after death and armed with this information I'm hoping and praying that you will be able to make a quality decision on the destiny of your future.

Once I heard he was in the hospital my wife and I went to visit with him not knowing about any of the circumstances that had occurred only a few days before. He was conscious when I arrived there but was very weak and he had to take his time telling me what had happened.

A few days before all of this took place I had read a book titled **"23 Minutes in Hell'** *by Bill Wiese*. It is one man's story about what he saw, heard, and felt in a place of terrible torment.

4 Faces of Death

Here is a quote from his book: *"My sincere hope is that this book is the closest you will ever come to experiencing Hell for yourself."*

Bill Wiese saw the searing flames of Hell, felt total isolation, and experienced the putrid and rotting stench, deafening screams of agony, terrorizing demons, and finally, the strong hand of God lifting him out of the pit saying, *"Tell them I am coming very, very soon!"*

I feel in my heart that the timing of this book being presented before me was a divinely appointed Word from God to speak to my friend as well as to many that are reading this book right now.

An Atheist's review of Bill was strongly tainted and bias with their doctrine that described him as a dreamer and a scammer who is only out to make money off his story which they feel is unbelievable to say the least.

This reminds me of a conversation I had one time when given the opportunity to speak to a man on death row; he tried to use the Bible to prove that God doesn't exist. I was amused by the fact that he didn't believe in God, and thought the Bible is only a book of fairy tales. Yet, he then wanted to use it to prove to me—there is no God. I told him you can't use a fairy-tale book to convince me there's no God.

He then told me of an experience that he had once: about going to a place in Hell. He said it was a scary place and his story sounded much like the testimony that Bill Wiese had shared about his encounter there.

He then cried out to a God (Who he doesn't believe in by the way) and said he was taken up out of that place by God and found himself back in his body. He then explained to me, he had taken a large dose of heroin right before all of this happened and explained that it was all just a hallucination induced by the overdose.

When you die you just stop existing, and that's it he said! I said well what if that were not true then where do you go? It sounds like you overdosed to me and died and God who loves you spared you an eternal place in Hell. I told him he just might want to reconsider his decision.

I have been in the prison ministry for close to thirty years and the testimonies of some of them who were executed without Christ in their lives; is that they died painful deaths. Some were screaming out that they were on fire and burning up. Some were screaming to get *'those devils'* away from them. *[Hey,*

4 Faces of Death

please don't get mad at me for reporting what happened to them. I had nothing to do with carrying out any of their executions.]

This man that I was talking to on death row called me a liar saying, no one is raised from the dead. He said there is no Heaven and/or no Hell. I knew his cell mate for over 25 years and told him that he had asked me to go to his execution saying; I've done everything in the prison ministry but that. I had absolutely no desire to go watch someone die, but out of respect for our friendship—I agreed to go.

When the time came for him to face that final curtain, he looked right at me with the greatest, biggest smile on his face, and said to me *"I'm going, I'm going,"* he repeated, and then he was gone.

There are lots of uneducated guesses by people who refuse to believe that we are created in the image of God. The man then asked me to give him just one ounce of evidence. He said if I could turn his toilet water into beer then he might believe. I asked him why beer? I had a hard time trying not to laugh at his ridiculous request.

It is always amazing, that when you throw God into the mix of your conversation just how mad people can get with you over something—that they say doesn't exist.

4 Faces of Death

Then this man told me that one day 'his savior,' (whose name is [death]) will deliver him from this hell he is living in. My response was even death will one day bow its knee to the Name of Jesus, he just smiled at me. Then I went my way with an invitation from him to come and talk with him on this subject again.

I told him that this was the best conversation I had all day, and he replied to me to please come back because he was extremely bored to death in his cell.

Well enough about that, lets get back to our testimony and see what we can find out about his experience that will enlighten us on this journey we are on.

I was told, when my friend came out of the induced comma some 10 days later, that the Lord had been dealing with him about three things: love, unforgiveness, and judging other people. He also told me several times that the Lord had told him—he needed to repent. He would begin to cry at this statement and needed a little time to regain his composer.

Setting next to his bed he began to tell Connie and I that he was at a dealership in Oklahoma City; so he could buy a truck for his business. He took the one he felt would work for him for a spin and once back at the dealership he began to feel funny and got into the back of his own truck and told his friend that went with him to take him to the hospital saying that something was wrong and that he was not feeling well.

He said *"I remember getting into the truck and the next thing I know I was in the back of what looked like a big gray prison bus. It was full of people that were handcuffed to their sets. They were all laughing and seemed to be having a good time. I wondered why I was on this bus."*

While he was sharing this information with me he started to cry again, but then he went on to say, *"I then found myself back in my truck once again and we had arrived at the hospital. I got out and they said that I had collapsed to the floor. And once again I found myself back on the bus. I looked out of the window and I saw a very large beehive just outside of the bus.*

"No one on the bus seemed to be concerned about why they were on it and shackled to their seats. Seeing the scene of a huge beehive just outside of the bus was not bothering them either."

Things get a little confusing at this point as he explained to me that he had died three times before they got him admitted into the hospital. He doesn't remember going into the hospital, but he did tell me that he died at the entrance of the hospital lobby where they then rushed him into ICU.

4 Faces of Death

Again he saw the prison bus, but this time he found himself standing outside of it watching the people climb up the side of this huge beehive. The beehive looked like it was lying on its side and people were climbing up the side of it and were dropping down into Hell as a dark figure was snatching their spirits right out of their bodies."

He was not sure why the Lord had shown him this chain of events, but he was seeking an answer to its mystery. He did say, the Lord looked at him and told him he could leave now and he ran away from there as fast as he could. I believe that God was wanting him to tell people about this horrible place called Hell. You may call it a fairytale place but one day you are going to find out that you threw away your last chance to escape it through your unbelief. *(See Scripture references p. 87)*

Bright Lights and Music
Written by Wayne Sanders

I have only one more testimony that I would like to add to those that have already be given and that is about my mother in law (Bernadine Smith).

We were living in Tulsa at the time when we received a call from my wife's stepfather saying we needed to come to Springfield, Mo. to see her mom. Things did not look favorable for her and she was slipping away fast. He said unless the man upstairs doesn't do something quickly—she will not make it. I have learned from past experiences,

4 Faces of Death

that when God is referred to as *'the man upstairs'* that the person saying it has little or no relationship with the Father, just saying.

So immediately we left for Missouri with the peace in our hearts that Bernadine was in good hands, both at the hospital and with God. She had made Jesus the Lord of her life a long time ago.

When we arrived my stepfather was very uneasy and you could see he was worried that he would lose her forever this time. She had been here in this position before but she never had the experience that happened with this encounter at the hospital. While she was lying on the operating table during the procedure the doctor was performing on her veins they found a large blood clot. The doctors told Don that it was near her temple and they were trying to dissolve the clot as slowly as possible. They said that if this blood clot breaks loose too soon that it would pass through her brain and it would result in her immediate death. Bernadine said that she was in the upper corner of the room looking down on them work on her body and that she could hear everything they were saying. Then she found herself in Heaven. *(See Scripture references p. 91)*

She told us that what she saw there was just out of this world. There were bright lights and music everywhere. *"I wanted to stay there because it was so peaceful. It was the most peaceful feeling that I have ever had in my life, but He wouldn't let me stay. I was told I had to go back; evidently I had more things that needed to be done."*

Don, (Connie's stepfather) later received Jesus into his heart and his last few years on this side of Heaven was awesome to see. We had just come back from a mission trip to Pennsylvania called: '**Fire on the Mountain**' and at the age of 84 she was sharing her faith with anyone that would [stop long enough to] hear what she had to say.

The Word Works

Written by Wayne Sanders, as told by the Pastor (father of Elijah)
Elijah Left for Dead: *Let me say this in hopes that you have no doubt where I stand as far as the bible is concerned. If it's a fairytale book like many claimed that it is, then why does it work in the lives of believers all around the world?*

Here is just one more testimony that I feel that needs to be shared within the pages of this book.

A message sent to God's people, "The Word Works" There is one testimony in particular that I want to share with you that inspired a church to come out from under the pressures of gang infested violence. They were walking with the authority given to them by Christ and they put the Word to work to set them free.

A pastor in the mountains of Honduras was troubled

4 Faces of Death

over his son who had left the church and was involved with the local gang. The son's activities with the gang brought much shame and embarrassment to this pastor, but it never once detoured his love for his son.

I need to go back a little in time to bring us up to date to this trip. In November, 2013 we were at the same church and the Spirit of God was moving in the service. The pastor saw some things that night that helped increase his faith.

As the pastor shared with us about his son we began to decree a thing as the Word says and God began to establish it. His son's name was Elijah and we called out to him to leave the gangs and return to the church. The faith of this father first, and then pastor, was strengthened even though he did not see the manifestation of those prayers until December, 2013 when Elijah returned home leaving the gang life behind him. *(See photo, p. 86)*

Elijah grew stronger in the Word as the months went by and on July 14, 2014, he was faced with a tremendous attack that would rock his faith in God's Word.

While getting ready for work at 6:00 am in the morning, he was taking a shower behind the church when he saw six men coming toward him all caring guns. He shouted at them *"Why do you want to kill me? I have done nothing to you."*

Four of the six men left and the remaining two men

walked up to him. Elijah's father had just preached a message that Sunday about putting on the armor of God. So Elijah started praying the blood of Jesus over himself and then started praying as he began dressing himself with the armor of God.

Ephesians 6:10-18
10 Finally, my brethren, be strong in the Lord, and in the power of his might.
11 Put on the whole armour of God, that ye may be able to stand against the wiles of the devil.
12 For we wrestle not against flesh and blood, but against principalities, against powers against the rulers of the darkness of of this world, against spiritual wickedness in high places.
13 Wherefore take unto you the whole armour of God, that ye may be able to withstand in the evil day, and having done all, to stand.
14 Stand therefore, having your loins girt about with truth, and having on the breastplate of righteousness;
15 And your feet shod with the preparation of the gospel of peace;
16 Above all, taking the shield of faith, wherewith ye shall be able to quench all the fiery darts of the wicked.
17 And take the helmet of salvation, and the sword of the Spirit, which is the word of God:
18 Praying always with all prayer and supplication in the Spirit, and watching thereunto with all perseverance and supplication for all saints;

4 Faces of Death

The two remaining men opened fire and shot him once in the neck where the bullet went in the front and exited out of the back. Then they shot him six times in the chest and left him lying on the floor of the shower bleeding to death.

He said that he was unconscious for what seemed like just a few minutes. He stood up, put a towel around his waist and started walking toward the highway to try to get a taxi to take him to the hospital.

A little girl saw him and brought him some sandals to walk across the rocks. There was blood everywhere and when he found a taxi driver he refused to let Elijah get into the car for fear of Elijah dying and then he would be sued. By this time the police where on the scene and the pastor (his father) arrived as well. The police ordered the taxi driver to take Elijah to the hospital.

When they arrived at a private clinic they refused to admit him without paying a huge amount of money as a down payment, $70,000 limperials, which is roughly around $3,300.00 in US dollars. The general hospital was at least another 40 minutes away from there and time was ticking away. They had no choice but to go there, but Elijah and his father were speaking out loud that he would live and not die and proclaim the Word of God.

Psalms 118:15-17 NIV
15 Shouts of joy and victory resound in the tents

of the righteous: "The Lord's right hand has done mighty things!
16 The Lord's right hand is lifted high; the Lord's right hand has done mighty things!"
17 I will not die but live, and will proclaim what the Lord has done.

Arriving at the hospital they immediately admitted him into the emergency room and were prepping him for surgery. With the huge loss of blood they were getting ready to give him some. Then came the real shocker.

The bullet that went through his neck missed his main artery and had not touched anything vital such as his spinal column or voice box. The only way they could explain the six shots in the chest was they just bounced off him like he was wearing a bullet-proof vest (the Breast Plate of Righteousness would be more like it).

They called him a walking miracle and released him to go back home. They never had to give him any blood even after the evidence of all the blood that he had lost.

Four of the six men are dead already. One of the men was walking down the street and a bolt of lightning struck him burning him up from head to toe. The fifth man is in prison, and they can't find the sixth one anywhere. My heart goes out to those that attacked him. Time is short and I pray that someone was able to speak to them about

4 Faces of Death

the saving grace of God before they lost their lives.

One year ago the church was leaving the services no later than 8:30 pm at night for fear of walking home in the dark. Now the fear is gone there and the joy that we felt in that church on this trip was, without saying, absolutely amazing.

(Epilogue)
In Closing...

The Word of God in the last verse of John's Gospel tells us Jesus Christ was truly—A MIRACLE MAN, THE ULTIMATE HEALER and THE WONDER WORKER.

John 21:25 KJV
And there are also many other things which Jesus did, the which, if they should be written every one, I suppose that even the world itself could not contain the books that should be written. Amen.

4 Faces of Death

This is Elijah's Father who is the pastor of the church
located in the mountains of Honduras,
who relayed the story to me.

4 Faces of Death

Scriptures about Hell

Matthew 25:30
And cast ye the unprofitable servant into **<u>outer darkness: there shall be weeping and gnashing of teeth</u>***"*

Luke 16:23-24
23 "And **<u>in hell</u>** *he lift up his eyes, being in torments, and seeth Abraham afar off, and Lazarus in his bosom.*
24 "And he cried and said, Father Abraham, have mercy on me, and send Lazarus, that he may dip the tip of his finger in water, and cool my tongue; for **<u>I am tormented in this flame.</u>***"*

▪ NOTE: The rich man wanted water but could not get any.

2 Samuel 22:6
"The **<u>sorrows of hell</u>** *compassed me about; the snares of death prevented me;"*

2 Thessalonians 1:9
"Who shall be **<u>punished with everlasting destruction from the presence of the Lord</u>***, and from the glory of his power;"*

Matthew 25:41
Then shall he say also unto them on the left hand, Depart from me, **<u>ye cursed, into ever-</u>**

**lasting fire, prepared for the devil and his angels:**

Isaiah 5:14
Therefore **hell hath enlarged herself, and opened her mouth without measure:** and their glory, and their multitude, and their pomp, and he that rejoiceth, shall descend into it.

Revelations 21:8
"But the fearful, and unbelieving, and the abominable, and murderers, and whoremongers, and sorcerers, and idolaters, and all liars, shall have their part in **the lake which burneth with fire and brimstone: which is the second death**"

Mark 9:43-44
43 "And if thy hand offend thee, cut it off: it is better for thee to enter into life maimed, than having two hands **to go into hell, into the fire that never shall be quenched:**
44 "Where their worm dieth not, and **the fire is not quenched**"

Psalms 9:17
The wicked shall be turned into hell, and all the nations that forget God.

Revelations 9:2
"And he opened **the bottomless pit; and there arose**

4 Faces of Death

a smoke out of the pit, as the smoke of a great furnace; and the sun and the air were darkened by reason of the smoke of the pit"

Revelations 14:11
"And the smoke of their torment ascendeth up for ever and ever: and they have no rest day nor night, who worship the beast and his image, and whosoever receiveth the mark of his name"

Matthew 22:13
Then said the king to the servants, Bind him hand and foot, and take him away, and cast him into outer darkness; there shall be weeping and gnashing of teeth"

Revelations 20:13-14
13 And the sea gave up the dead which were in it; and death and hell delivered up the dead which were in them: and they were judged every man according to their works.
14 "And death and hell were cast into the lake of fire. This is the second death"

4 Faces of Death

4 Faces of Death

Scriptures about Heaven

Genesis 14:22
And Abram said to the king of Sodom, I have lift up mine hand unto the LORD, the most high God, the possessor of **heaven** *and earth,*

Matthew 6:20
"But **lay up for yourselves treasures in heaven, where neither moth nor rust doth corrupt,** *and where thieves do not break through nor steal:"*

Luke 6:23
Rejoice ye in that day, and leap for joy: for, behold, **your reward is great in heaven:** *for in the like manner did their fathers unto the prophets.*

Revelations 19:1
And after these things I heard **a great voice of much people in heaven,** *saying, Alleluia; Salvation, and glory, and honour, and power, unto the Lord our God:*

Genesis 28:12
And he dreamed, and behold a ladder set up on the earth, and **the top of it reached to heaven:** *and behold the angels of God ascending and descending on it.*

Revelations 4:2
And immediately I was in the spirit: and, behold, **a throne was set in heaven, and one sat on the throne.**

4 Faces of Death

2 Corinthians 12:2
I knew a man in Christ above fourteen years ago, (whether in the body, I cannot tell; or whether out of the body, I cannot tell: God knoweth;) such an one **caught up to the third heaven.**

Deuteronomy 4:39
Know therefore this day, and consider it in thine heart, that the LORD **he is God in heaven above,** *and upon the earth beneath: there is none else.*

Ephesians 3:15
Of whom **the whole family in heaven** *and earth is named,*

Mark 16:19
So then after the Lord had spoken unto them, he was **received up into heaven,** *and sat on the right hand of God.*

2 Kings 2:11b
...there appeared a chariot of fire, and horses of fire, and parted them both asunder; and Elijah **went up by a whirlwind into heaven.**

Luke 10:20
Notwithstanding in this rejoice not, that the spirits are subject unto you; but rather rejoice, because **your names are written in heaven.**

4 Faces of Death

1 Peter 1:4
*To an inheritance incorruptible, and undefiled, and that fadeth not away, **reserved in heaven for you,***

Revelations 21:14
*And **the wall of the city had twelve foundations,** and in them the names of the twelve apostles of the Lamb.*

Revelations 21:21-27
*21 And the twelve gates were twelve pearls; every several gate was of one pearl: and **the street of the city was pure gold, as it were transparent glass.***
22 And I saw no temple therein: for the Lord God Almighty and the Lamb are the temple of it.
*23 And **the city had no need of the sun, neither of the moon, to shine in it: for the glory of God did lighten it,** and the Lamb is the light thereof.*
24 And the nations of them which are saved shall walk in the light of it: and the kings of the earth do bring their glory and honour into it.
25 And the gates of it shall not be shut at all by day: for there shall be no night there.
26 And they shall bring the glory and honour of the nations into it.
27 And there shall in no wise enter into it any thing that defileth, neither whatsoever worketh abomination, or maketh a lie: but they which are written in the Lamb's book of life.

4 Faces of Death

Prayer for Salvation

Lord God, I know I am guilty and do not deserve your mercy. I also understand that You loved the world so much. That you loved ME so much, that you sent Your only Son to die on a cross, and pay the price for my sin. I believe there is nothing that I can do to earn Your forgiveness, and I recognize it is a free gift from You. I believe and confess with my mouth that Jesus Christ is Your Son, Messiah, Savior of the World. I believe in my heart You raised Jesus from the dead. I ask you to forgive my sins entirely. I confess today that I will dedicate the remainder of my life to serving and obeying Your Word and Your ways, with Jesus Christ as my Lord. I thank You that according to your Word (the Bible), I can be assured that I am saved from Hell and will spend eternity in Heaven with You!

Thank you, Father!
In Jesus' Name, Amen!

John 3:16
For God so loved the world that He gave His only begotten Son, that whoever believes in Him should not perish but have everlasting life. For God sent not His Son into the world to condemn the world, but that the world, through Him, might be saved.

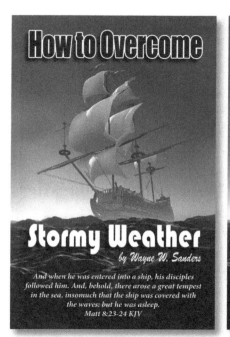

Enjoy these other great books from Bold Truth Publishing

Seemed Good to THE HOLY GHOST
by Daryl P Holloman

I Have a Story to Tell
by Jean Carlburg

Obedience is Not an Option
by Brian Ohse

TURN OFF THE STEW
by Judy Spencer

KINGDOM of LIGHT 1 - kingdom of darkness
Truth about Spiritual Warfare
by Minister Michael R. Hicks

The Holy Spirit SPEAKS Expressly
by Elizabeth Pruitt Sloan

Matthew 4:4
Man shall not live by bread alone,
but by every word that proceedeth out of the mouth of God.
by Rick McKnight

Supernatural Guidance
by Prophet Ronnie Moore

The ROAD TO THE PROMISE
Learn how to find purpose in the process
by Prophetess Candace Rivera

VICTIM TO VICTOR
THE CHOICE IS YOURS
by Rachel V. Jeffries

THE GIFT of KNOWING Our Heavenly Father
Abiding in Intimacy
by Deborah K. Reed

SEEING BEYOND
by Kelly Taylor Nutt

SPIRITUAL BIRTHING
Bringing God's Plans & Purposes and Manifestation
by Lynn Whitlock Jones

BECOMING PERFECT
Let The Perfector Perfect His Work In You
by Sally Stokes Weiesnbach

FIVE SMOOTH STONES
by Aaron Jones

■▪■▪■▪■▪■▪■▪■▪■▪■▪■▪■▪■▪■▪■▪■▪■

■ Spanish Books / Libros españoles

▪ El Búho Sabio y Viejo
El Lenguaje Celestial
por Marcella O'Banion Burnes

▪ Como Superar La Tempestad
por Wayne W. Sanders

Available at Select Bookstores and at
www.BoldTruthPublishing.com

The hurt, lonely, oppressed and "called" are the heart-beat of prison ministry. The VICTORY is being able to reach out, touch another life and make a POSITIVE difference for the Glory of God!

A MUST READ – PRACTICAL TEACHING GIVING YOU A STRATEGY FOR FINDING "HIDDEN TREASURE" IN PRISON MINISTRY.

Available at select bookstores and
www.BoldTruthPublishing.com